CHRONICLES
of a
JOURNEY

EMBRACING PAIN ON MY PATH TO SELF-DISCOVERY

Copyright © 2017 by Ricardo Palomares. All rights reserved. Printed in the United States of America. No part of this publication may be reproduced, distributed, or transmitted in any form or by any means, including photocopying, recording, or other electronic or mechanical methods, without written permission of the publisher, except in the case of brief quotations embodied in reviews and certain other non-commercial uses permitted by copyright law. For information, see www.ricardopal.com.

Library of Congress Cataloguing-in-Publication Data

Ricardo Palomares
Chronicles of a Journey: Embracing Pain on my Path to Self-Discovery

ISBN: 9781521336366

Interior designed by www.writingnights.org

Dedication

To God, who has always been there when I needed Him the most. Even when I thought He had forgotten me, He was always guiding me toward what I needed at that exact moment, even when it came in the form of pain.

Table of Contents

Dedication III

Table of Contents V

Acknowledgements VII

Introduction VIII

Chapter One — A Dream 1

Chapter Two — Sacrifices 9

Chapter Three — The Starting Point 20

Chapter Four — Accepting the Consequences 35

Chapter Five — One Step at a Time 42

Chapter Six — Love Yourself for Who You Are 58

Chapter Seven — Strengths, not Weaknesses 69

Chapter Eight — Learn to Love the Pain 78

Chapter Nine — Everything is Temporary 92

Chapter Ten — A New Dream 100

Let's Work Together 106

Acknowledgements

I want to acknowledge all the people who believed I could accomplish what I set out to do.

I especially want to thank all my mentors who saw something in me I didn't see at the time. They believed in me when I did not yet believe in myself. Thank you, Winfield and Karen Little, Howie Nestel, Leanne Valenti, and Alberto Trueba.

Thank you to my editor, Elayne Wells Harmer, for honoring my voice while clarifying my message.

To my mom, Angelica, and my dad, Alejandro. Even though they did not fully understand what I was trying to accomplish, they still supported me in following my dreams.

To my brothers, Alejandro and Carlos, who have always inspired me to pursue art, no matter what.

Introduction

Some of the best memories of my childhood are watching movies with my family, sitting down in the living room cuddled next to my mom, wrapped up in a blanket and sipping hot chocolate. My mom loved mysteries where detectives had to solve crimes; somehow she was always the first to guess who did it. Sometimes that made me feel dumb, since it usually took me until the last minute to figure things out.

I also remember watching movies with my oldest brother in his room. He would record all his favorites movies from TV onto old VHS tapes, and just about every day we'd watch movies together while he drew. Alejandro is an artist, and he would draw comic books for hours.

There was something so magical about spending time in my brother's room—I felt like I was in another world where anything was possible. On one side of the room, my brother drew stories where limits didn't exist, and on the other side I had the TV showing me worlds I had never seen or even imagined. In those movies, characters had the ability to achieve the impossible.

In a way, movies protected me and made me feel safe from having to deal with my parents' constant fighting, and eventually their divorce. My brothers and I stayed with my mom, and we struggled a lot financially. Movies helped me forget we were poor; for a few brief hours, the troubles we had to make ends meet disappeared. Watching movies helped me believe there was a place out there where one day I would feel like I belonged. Movies helped me trust that there was a unique purpose for my life, and that I had within me the faith and will to fulfill that purpose.

For as long as I can remember, I've dreamed about being an explorer who would travel around the world, living epic adventures and helping people along the way. My mom stayed at home, taking care of us kids. I didn't have an example of adventure in my life, nor did I have the money to pursue it even if I had.

Movies helped me feel like I wasn't crazy to dream. I believed I actually had a chance to achieve my dream—if I just pursued it with everything I had.

My favorite movie is *Gattaca*, a science fiction story set in a not-too-distant future, where babies are created and genetically enhanced in a laboratory and then placed in a womb. Doctors make sure these babies won't be afflicted with diabetes, myopia, baldness, or any other illnesses or deformities. The main character, Vincent, is conceived the old-fashioned way, and so is born with myopia, heart disease, and other biological imperfections. His dream is to become an astronaut, but in that alternate future, jobs depend on how good your genes are, and Vincent's genes aren't good. He knows he can't become an astronaut unless he relies on someone else's genetic testing.

Just before the final scene, Vincent and his brother Anton, who is genetically enhanced, swim into the ocean for a game. When they were kids, they often played a game of "chicken" to see who would swim the farthest before turning back. In this scene, just before Anton gives up and concedes the race, he asks Vincent how he had achieved so much despite being physically imperfect.

"You want to know how I did it?" Vincent asks. "I never saved anything for the swim back."

I see myself in Vincent, and I understand his struggle. For two decades, I have sacrificed everything in my life. I left my home, my friends, my family, and my country. I have endured loneliness and being broke and homeless. I have overcome depression and major physical injuries. I've done all that for one dream: experiencing the adventure of seeing the world. I never saved anything for the swim back.

There's a deep part of me that knows there is so much beauty to see, and the most important part of my dream is to share that beauty. I truly believe this is my contribution to the world: to show that even though people from different countries and cultures have differences, we are more similar than most people think.

After 20 years, I finally get to say that I am living my dream—to explore the world and tell stories about it. I want to show people what is out there, so they can realize what is possible.

This book is about my story, and the things I have learned along the way. This book is about a kid who went from having nothing but a big dream, to traveling around the world doing what he loves. I want to share my story with you because I believe that within each of us lies the ability, faith, strength, talent, determination, grit, love, and compassion to achieve our greatest dreams, even when they seem impossible.

I believe we all have a life purpose we need to fulfill, and hopefully this book will encourage, motivate, and inspire you to take action. I am sharing my story because I believe you can become more than you think, and that your spirit is greater than any obstacle you encounter along the way.

Chapter
– One –
A Dream

I WAS BORN JANUARY 25, 1982, IN MEXICO CITY, a twin and the youngest of four boys. Even as babies, my twin brother and I had very different personalities. Angel had a lighthearted temperament and was curious and adventurous. He simply had no fear. I, on the other hand, was completely the opposite: afraid of everything, hesitant, and unsure of myself.

My mom tells stories of Angel looking for adventure while I tried to talk him out of it—and that was when we were just starting to walk. Even at that age I was already cautious and restrained. Angel was active and too busy to eat, but I was more sedentary and loved food. My mom says that I used to drink my baby bottle, then steal Angel's and drink his, too. My mom calls me "Gordo"

("Fatso") to this day—I'm no longer a chubby toddler, but the nickname stuck.

My brother and I were like Danny DeVito and Arnold Schwarzenegger in the movie *Twins*, where Arnold's character gets all the good genes and Danny's character gets all the leftovers. Our differences also remind me of the brothers in *Gattaca*, where Anton is genetically enhanced and Vincent is just average.

But despite our different personalities and body types, we were inseparable. My mom says we were best friends, even as toddlers. Angel and I spent virtually every waking hour together, and we balanced each other out. He came up with the adventures, and I made sure we would get out of them safely.

After our adventures, we would eat grapes side by side in the backyard. We spit the seeds out into the dirt, and eventually two grape trees grew right in that spot. Side by side, just like us.

But one day when we were two years old, Angel went exploring without me. Our nanny was taking care of all four boys, and somehow in the chaos of our playing, Angel escaped without anyone noticing. He found a bottle of floor-cleaning liquid and did what any curious little boy would do: he drank it.

The acid in the cleaner burned Angel's throat, and he had to be fed through a tube for months. He seemed to be getting better for a while, but then one day the doctors said he needed surgery. It was just a minor thing, they said—nothing to be worried about. My mother was shocked when the surgeon came out to tell her that Angel had not survived.

He was just two—such a short life for such a beautiful soul. I wish I had memories of him. I wish I remembered his face. I wish I could remember how it feels to have a constant companion.

My mom told me that after Angel passed away, she would often hear me laugh by myself in the room we had shared. She would come into my room to see what I was doing, and I would explain, "I'm playing with my brother!" Somehow, we were still connected, and my mom says I often acted as if Angel were still physically present. My mom says that at times I would act like I could see him.

During that difficult time, my mom prayed to God to let her see her little boy just one more time. After a while, God answered her prayers. She told me that one day she saw Angel and me playing together in our backyard—Angel was sitting on our swing and I was pushing him. She saw him for a bit, and then he disappeared.

I don't remember any of that. Thinking back to life with my twin brother is kind of foggy, like it happened in another life or to someone else. When I see photos of us together, I do get a feeling of familiarity, kind of like when I go back home after a long trip. It doesn't matter how much you change during a journey—you still remember where you came from.

What I do remember is that for a long time I felt a hole in the center of my chest, an emptiness that nothing could really fill. For a long time I felt like something was missing. I remember thinking of him every day as I grew up, wondering what life would be like if he were still with me. I wondered what activities he would like. My mom says he was really good at kicking balls; Angel had "soccer player legs," she'd say. I guess that's the dream of every Mexican mom—to have a good soccer player for a son.

Some time after my brother died, my personality started to change. Some of the fear left, along with doubt and hesitation. I started to be more curious, too. I started to wonder about a lot of things, especially the world. I gradually became braver and more adventurous. I would play in the mountains in front of my home for hours, all by myself. Most of the time I spent daydreaming about becoming an explorer and taking unforgettable journeys. A massive love of exploration started to build up inside me, and nothing else made me happier.

During this time, one of our grape trees in the backyard started weakening, and eventually only the other tree survived. Sometimes I wonder if my brother was giving me a little push: one tree died to make the other stronger.

My family says they see in me a lot of the traits that Angel had. They think he would probably do the things I do. I'm not sure how I absorbed some of his qualities, but maybe it was my way to compensate for his absence, to subconsciously honor him. To be honest, there are times when I feel like I have two completely different personalities. One is extremely confident, the other more restrained. In a way, I feel like I am living a life for both Angel and me. One reason I've devoted my life to exploring the world is because I think that's what my brother would have done. This is a life I can share with him.

At some point when I was young, I started noticing my dad's *National Geographic* magazines. He had dozens of them, since he'd been a huge fan long before I was born. Going through those magazines fueled my need to travel. They were fascinating, and opened up a world that was completely new to me. I was shocked to realize how vast and magnificent the earth really is.

I was fascinated by the stories, but the photos pulled me in even more. I wondered what it would be like to be the photographer. *How would it feel to be there?* I would think in amazement. How would it feel to be in the middle of the forest interacting with gorillas, or in the streets of China capturing the underground culture? I longed to know how it would feel to be in that exact moment, in that specific place, capturing that experience, so involved in the moment that for a second you are no longer a spectator but part of the landscape.

A couple of months before I graduated from high school, I still had no idea what was I going to do with my life. I had no plan for how to become a world traveler. The only thing I knew is that I had to go to college, because that's what my family expected from me. I had no idea what I was going to study; I doubted I could major in "Exploration."

One day as I was walking back home from school, I started wondering about my future. At the moment there was no clear path, or at least none of the options sounded good. I asked myself out loud, "What do you want?" My response was immediate: "I want to travel the world, doing what I love."

At the time, I didn't really know what "doing what I love" meant. I loved exploring around the mountain by my house, but I didn't think I could actually become an explorer as a career. I needed to learn some kind of skill. But then my mind connected the dots: if I did something I loved, my passion for it would make me great at it, and because I'd become so great, that skill would take me around the world. The answer came to me in a flash.

"Photography!" I exclaimed out loud.

Just like that, I decided I was going to travel around the world as a photographer. I somehow knew, without doubt or hesitation, that being a photographer would lead me to become an explorer. My dream became crystal clear: I would travel around the world, doing what I love.

As important as it was to have focused my dream into a plan, I knew I needed a powerfu needed an ultimate purpose. Just as quickly as photography had popped into my mind, I instinctively knew that I wanted to honor my brother's life by telling stories worth sharing. I wanted to use my camera to help people understand the world, to see the connection and similarities between us. I believe that when we understand what we have in common, it helps us understand who we are.

I have a vivid memory of that moment, the day I walked home from school and knew with clarity what I wanted to do and why. Having such a powerful reason has given me the fire and determination to endure a couple of decades of overcoming massive obstacles, and has left me no option but to accomplish my dreams.

CHAPTER
– *Two* –
SACRIFICES

I REMEMBER THE DAY MY MOM TOLD US THAT she and my dad were getting a divorce. She said they wanted to wait until my brothers and I were old enough to handle it. My first thought was, *Thank God, it's about time!* My parents fought constantly growing up, so a divorce sounded like a blessing.

My brothers and I stayed with my mom, and my dad moved out. That was when things started to get really bad. We were constantly struggling to make ends meet. My dad was helping us as much as he could, and we were trying our best, but every month it seemed like we were not going to make it. We had the electricity and water shut off more than once, but my mom always figured out how to put food on the table.

Around that time, I started to look for a photography school, and I soon found one near my house. I checked it out, talked to the admissions office, and everything looked great. Of course, chasing my dream couldn't be that easy, right? It turned out I didn't have the only thing I needed to get in: money.

When I went after my dreams, at first I thought that just showing up was going to be enough, that a good attitude would get me there. But I for sure could not pay for school with just a good attitude.

That was when I truly started to understand the sacrifices my dreams were going to require. To be honest, if I had known everything I would go through in the following 15 years, I wouldn't have begun pursuing my dreams. On the other hand, knowing the immediate sacrifices pushed me to focus, and being aware of the sacrifices forced me to take my dreams seriously. It lit a fire within me that burned for the next 15 years.

I found just enough money to enroll for the first term, and then I found three different jobs so I could pay for the rest.

My first job was being a dragon for kid events. Most dragon costumes have at least two different parts to it: the head and the body. Mine wasn't like that. I don't know who designed the stupid thing, but the one I had to wear was only one giant piece—one massive dragon, with one pair of enormous wings and a long tail.

I'm no costume designer, but I would think that a key thing to consider when designing a costume would be how in the heck people are going to put the dang thing on! I had to lay the dragon on the floor, crawl into it, find the holes where my arms were supposed to go, and say, "Ready!" to let my two friends know when to pull me up. After that, I had to put on two giant dragon feet. Both the shoes and the costume smelled equally bad.

Because the dragon costume would get so crazy hot, I had to attach a battery to an internal fan, which didn't work most of the time. Saying that it was extremely uncomfortable is an understatement. For one hour, I would stand in the front door wearing a stinky ginormous dragon costume, carrying what looked like a car battery to power a fan that didn't work, and saying hi to kids who were too horrified to say hi back.

My second job was as a bartender in an old bohemian bar.

"I saw you have an opening as a bartender," I told the manager as soon as I walked in. "Now, I have no idea how to bartend, but I learn really fast!"

"You're in!" he replied.

I learned to tend bar and eventually took over the main bartender's job, because he was too drunk to serve drinks most of the time.

Once we were done with work, my friends and I would get together and play soccer, sometimes till sunrise. At that time there was no public transportation, so it would take me an hour to walk back home. I remember one time I was so tired that I fell asleep while I was walking. I was literally sleepwalking.

My third job was taking photos of soccer and basketball games. That was my very first job as a photographer, but I'm not too sure if it counts as a job, because I was losing money most of the time. I guess my dream back then was not to become a great businessman!

At the time, I was head over heels in love with a girl named Mariana. She played basketball and soccer, so every weekend I had the opportunity to watch her. Mariana and I kissed a couple of times, but nothing more ever happened. I remember the day she told me she was going to play her last game of high school soccer. I got there just in time to catch the last part of the game, saw her score a goal, took her photo on the field, and then left without saying goodbye.

A regular Friday looked like this: I woke up at 8 and I'd get to school by 9. After school, I'd go straight to work as a dragon, and immediately afterward head over to the bar and work till 3 in the morning. Then, of course, I'd play soccer for a bit. After that, I'd walk to my house (or "sleepwalk" to my house). I'd shower and get dressed, then head out to take photos till 3 p.m. Saturday.

I would be awake for more than 30 hours straight. That's not sustainable at all, just in case you didn't know, or are curious about trying it. Don't. It was one of the hardest times in my life. I pushed myself like I never had before.

After months and months, this schedule really took a toll on me. At times I felt so defeated, tired, and exhausted. At times I was completely drained. It felt like I was in a really long dream, where everything was foggy. There were times when my mind couldn't think anymore. I would sit down to eat with my family and stare at the plate of food, lost in my exhaustion. My mom would ask if I was ok, and I would respond "yes" almost automatically, without even knowing what the question was in the first place. I would tell myself, *You can do this, you can do this, you can do this...*

I guess I was trying to convince myself that I could do it, without knowing if I really could.

One day is branded in my heart, when something happened that helped me believe that what seemed impossible *was* possible. This experience convinced me I could do what I had set out to do.

It was almost midnight, and I was working at the bar, completely exhausted. This was one of those times when everything seemed foggy, when it felt like I was in a really long dream. By that time, I had already worked 16 hours. I still had at least four more hours to go before the bar closed. I was serving drinks and could barely focus, so I took a break and hid in the back of the kitchen. I leaned my back against a fridge and collapsed to the ground. My head was hiding between my knees, and I started to cry uncontrollably.

Everything seemed too much; I was overwhelmed. It wasn't just that I was trying to pay for school by working non-stop; it was also that I was trying to deal with not knowing whether we would have electricity at home the next day. It seemed that everything was constantly against us—

both my family and me personally. I just felt like there was always something going wrong. It felt like there was no way for us to get ahead.

Why is life so hard? I asked myself. *Why is following my dreams so difficult?* I couldn't understand why just being alive was so challenging. It made me question what I was doing, and made me think hard about my dreams. I wondered if all this was worth it, and whether I was even going to accomplish my goals at all.

But for some reason, suddenly I pictured myself traveling around the world having epic adventures. I guess I was trying to make myself feel better. I imagined myself climbing Everest, capturing wildlife in Africa, and hiking up to Machu Picchu. That vision calmed me down and gave me a little bit of hope.

Do I really want my dreams this bad? I asked myself. The answer was a definite YES.

If I have to go through all these struggles to achieve my dreams, I can do this and more, I said to myself.

Of all the times I told myself I could do something, this one felt different, because this time I believed it. It was not me trying to *convince* myself I could do it; it was me telling myself there was no doubt I could.

That was one of the most powerful moments in my life, because it made me realize that only two things could ever stop me: God, and myself.

I truly believe that. Only two forces can potentially put obstacles on the path to our dreams. The first is God: nature, the universe, or a higher power, if you will. I believe if we pursue something that goes against a higher purpose or against the benefit of others or ourselves, we will always encounter friction in our journey. I also think God puts obstacles in our path to test us and see if we really want what we say we want.

The second force that has the power to stop us is our own self. The biggest obstacle we have to conquer is ourselves; we are only as capable as we believe we are.

After two years of going through this daily struggle, just before I finished photography school, I got a call from my Aunt Paty. She told me that Winn, my dad's cousin, was a photographer in San Antonio, Texas. Paty knew I was going to photography school and thought it would be a good idea to see if he could help me.

As soon as I heard that, I knew this was my chance to get closer to my dreams. Out of the blue, I called Winn.

"Hi, I'm Ricardo, your cousin's son," I said. "I heard that you're a photographer, and I'm just about to finish photography school. Do you think you could help me out?"

Amazingly, he said yes. Just like that, I decided to leave everything I knew behind, and I moved to San Antonio.

For most of my life until then, I'd had trouble making decisions, and having options made me uncomfortable. But choosing to move to the U.S. was effortless, because it was the first time in my life where it was clear what I had to do—maybe because it was the only option. It was the first time I had no doubt what I wanted.

The day I left home was completely different from what I expected. For years, I had imagined the day I would finally leave home to follow my dreams. I imagined family members and friends saying goodbye at the airport, telling me they were excited for me and that they were so proud. I thought there would be a party with friends holding signs that read, "I'll see you when I see you!"

The day I left was nothing like that. There was no party, there were no signs, no family members or friends waving at me as I boarded the plane. I woke up alone that morning at my mom's house. I think she was visiting family at the time, and I'm not sure where my brothers were.

I was listening to the soundtrack of *Gattaca* while I waited for the clock to let me know it was time to leave. The song I was listening to was from the scene when Vincent decides to leave home to pursue his dream of becoming an astronaut. I thought it was really fitting.

When it was time, I nervously left the house that would never be my home again. I went to my dad's apartment to pick up my bag. He wasn't there either, so I took a cab to the Mexico City airport by myself. I checked my bag, which had nothing in it but a few clothes, and walked to my gate. I sat down and opened up my backpack, and was happy to find a packet of crackers that Mariana had given me a couple of days earlier. I had given her my favorite Radiohead album, along with a letter that pointed out my favorite song: "True Love Waits." I ate those crackers as slowly as I could, since they were the last things that still connected me to my life in Mexico. As soon as I finished the last one, I heard the call to board the plane. I found my seat and put away my backpack. Looking out the window, I realized that I was leaving my old self and my old life behind.

I have never felt as lonely as I did on that flight. That was the day I knew that my path would probably be a lonely one, but my dreams would bring me as much fulfillment as loneliness. That flight to Texas was a reminder of the sacrifices I had made to get to that point, and I knew that I would make many more. That day was a reminder that all of it was worth it.

Chapter Three

The Starting Point

I LEFT HOME FOR ONLY THE SECOND TIME IN MY life on August 6, 2004. I remember the exact date because for a while I kept the plane ticket, next to my return flight ticket that I never used. The first time I left home had been four years earlier. My mom was really angry at my brother for something I thought was nothing to be mad about. Without anybody noticing, I snuck out of the house and went to spend the night with a friend. In my mind, I was leaving home.

The next morning, I realized that I didn't have the courage to go through with it, and I thought the best thing to do would be to go back home with my tail between my legs. My dad opened the door with a concerned look on his face, and told me he had been looking for me the whole night. I walked up the stairs and saw my mom. She made a beeline to me, and without hesitation—and with a look on her face I had never seen before—sternly said, "The next time you leave home, have the balls to leave and never come back!" She then turned around and walked away. I was speechless. My mom had a really unique way to teach us character.

The second time I left home, I made sure to never go back. For the first couple of years I lived with Winn, my dad's cousin. At the time, he and his wife, Karen, were really successful wedding photographers, and I became their assistant. They spent the next two years mentoring me. To be honest, I didn't know I needed to be mentored, but I sure did. I think maybe they saw something in me, some potential I couldn't see for myself. Even though I knew exactly what I wanted, in so many ways I was not ready to get it.

Those two years I lived with them felt like a boot camp. For the first couple of months, everything was exciting and new—but then everything started to settle. Suddenly I missed what I had left behind; I missed who I had been before. Not only did I leave everything I knew behind, I also left who I was. I found myself trying to adapt to a new environment while trying to figure out who I really was. Nobody told me that following my dreams was going to entail a lot of self-discovery, or that it would be so hard and lonely.

Winn was really tough with me; it seemed like everything I did was wrong. I hated him for months. I hated that he would even correct the way I walked. I remember one time he called me to his office and told me to come have dinner at their house. He had an office in a nice building in San Antonio, and I would sometimes stay there working till two or three in the morning. When I got back home, we sat down at the table. Out of the blue, he told me he was tired of me. To be fair, I probably deserved it. I'm not sure what I did to make him mad, but I'm sure I did *something*.

He said I acted like he was the one who needed me, instead of the other way around. He said I acted like I was entitled, and he wouldn't tolerate that.

"I want you to tell me how come you think you're valuable to my business," he said. I spent the next half-hour trying to sell myself as the best employee. Winn kept quiet the entire time, and when I was done he looked at me, and with no emotion, said he was not convinced. Then he said that he would no longer be teaching me, helping me, or mentoring me. I could still stay at his home if I wanted, but otherwise I was on my own.

To pay for community college, I worked as a parking valet and a waiter, and I waxed floors. I think Winn was expecting me to go back to Mexico, but when he saw that I didn't, he decided to help me again. He said he recognized that I had "grit." I think I just never thought there was an Option B.

As tough as those two years were, they were also formative. I see my life before and after my time with Winn and Karen. At the time I didn't know it, but that was the biggest act of love anybody has ever done for me. They taught me how to earn my dreams, and how to be a man. They taught me that everything necessary to achieve what seemed impossible was already within me. One day I asked Winn how I could ever pay him back.

"Do the same for someone else," he said.

At the time, I was living in a house under construction that Winn and Karen had bought to make into office space. They had asked me to move there to take care of it. It was during the winter, and I had nothing but a mattress on the floor to sleep on. There was no hot water, either, so when I wanted to take a shower, I would turn on the freezing water, close my eyes, and breathe deeply a couple of times before jumping in. Then I would scrub my entire body as quickly as I could.

One day a couple of years later, when construction was almost done, Winn told me it was time for me to "spread my wings" and move out—that very day. It was kind of a curveball, to be honest, but now I understand he did it so I could learn how to take care of myself. For some reason, humans are not wired to do most things until we are forced to. Most of the times when I overcame major obstacles, I did it mostly because I had no option but to overcome them.

The first couple of nights, I slept in my car. Then a friend let me sleep in his living room until I was able to pay rent for my own place. I spent the next couple of years making things happen. I became a wedding photographer for a while, then started a small ad agency with a couple of friends. I taught myself web design and graphic design.

For a while it felt like I was going down the wrong path, like I had forgotten why I left home. Suddenly, things had become about just surviving, not following my dreams. One day I asked myself,

What's the best-case scenario if I continue on this path? I realized the likely result would be to have a lot of clients, make a lot of money, and get stuck in San Antonio. That sounded awful.

Without hesitation, I decided to move on. My goal had never been to stay in one place—at least, not before I had traveled the world. It was then I decided to go to film school at the University of Texas at Austin. I wanted to tell stories in a more dynamic way, and I thought filmmaking could be the path. Once again, I left everything to start from scratch in another city, all to pursue my dreams.

My friend Manny and I left San Antonio together and rented an apartment in Austin. It reminded me of the house under construction where I used to live, because for a while we only had mattresses on the floor. At the time, both of us made money freelancing web design.

Once we were settled, I went to the admissions office at UT Austin to figure out what I needed to do to get in. One of the women in the office told me there was no way I could attend the school with a work visa, which is what I had at the time. She told me I needed a student visa, and after drilling her with questions, she firmly said that was the only way I was going to get in.

I left the office enraged. I thought to myself, "She doesn't get to tell me what I can and can't do!" I went back the next day and waited for the woman to leave the office. As soon as she left, I walked in and asked someone else what I needed to apply. I filled out all the information (again), and when the man asked about my visa, I told him I had the right type. He didn't question me further. I'm not sure if the woman was wrong or if the man didn't know what type of visa I needed, but I got accepted. When I left, I made sure the woman didn't see me.

I got accepted to UT Austin *and* to the film program, both of which are hard to do. Once I got in, I realized I was going to have to pay as an international student, which is three times more than regular tuition. It was around $15,000 per semester, and there was no way I could pay that. I talked to the admission office and asked them for advice, but I couldn't find any solution, so I lost my spot at school.

It was so frustrating that just getting an education could be so hard. At the end of the day, I just wanted to learn. On top of that, the admissions office told me that if I didn't register, I would have to re-apply, and it was likely that I wouldn't get accepted again, either to UT Austin or to the film program.

For the next year I focused on my new plan, which I called "Mission Impossible": Get accepted to UT Austin and the film program (again), get a scholarship that would let me pay the first semester as a resident, get a better work visa that would let me pay as a resident for the following semesters, and finally, get scholarships so I didn't have to pay for school at all. When I told Manny my plan, he thought it was ridiculous.

Around the same time, my car died. It literally just stopped working, and fixing it was more expensive than what it was worth. So "Mission Impossible" became a little bit more impossible. I looked on Craigslist for a cheap car and found an old white Pathfinder for $2,000. To be honest, $2,000 was way over my budget. Actually, I had no budget at all.

Martin was the guy selling the car. I emailed him to say I didn't have any money, but I knew how to do a lot of things. I asked him if he was willing to barter his car for my services.

"Yes, come see me," he wrote.

I arrived at a four-acre property with one main house and three run-down trailers. It turned out that Martin worked in construction, and the entire property was full of construction material. He also had chickens and other animals.

The property was on the outskirts of the city. We talked about the car and my services, and we agreed that I would build him a website in exchange for the car. I couldn't believe I pulled that off; I realized that I'm really good at bartering. As I was leaving his home, he pointed out one of the trailers.

"If you ever need a place to stay, let me know," he said. I told him thanks, but I already had a place to stay with my friend.

A couple of days later, my friend Manny told me he was moving back to San Antonio with his family. As soon as he said that, I thought about Martin and his offer. I called him and asked if he was willing to let me live in one of the trailers in exchange for help cleaning his property.

"Sure," he said. I thought to myself, *I just pulled this off, too?* But even more valuable than my skill at bartering was the kindness of Martin. For the next eight months, I lived in one of his trailers.

I had a car and a place to live, so now I needed to focus on "Mission Impossible": How to get accepted to UT Austin and pay for it. When we focus entirely on one thing, we start attracting that into our life—and most of the time, it's in ways we never would have expected. That's why when I want something, I just focus on what I want and not necessarily on how I'm going to get it, because I believe the way will present itself.

I was still freelancing web design while I lived at the trailer. Wanting to meet more people in Austin, I joined a Meetup group for web designers. During one of the meetings, a guy told me he'd graduated from the UT Austin film program. After hearing my story, he told me to go talk to the head of the communications department, who was a good friend of his.

A week later I met with the head of Communications, and told him how I had lost my spot and was looking to re-apply. I showed him my web design and photography portfolio.

"This is amazing!" he said, extremely impressed. "You need to be in this school!"

He told me to let him know when I submitted my application, because he would call the admissions office to tell them I was a great investment. So I re-applied, and I got accepted to both UT Austin and the film program again.

The next step was to figure out how to pay as a resident instead of as an international student. There was a program for Mexicans to pay as residents if they go to a school near the border. I applied for the second time and got it.

That took care of the first semester, but I still had to figure out how to pay as a resident for the following semesters. The only way I could do that was to get a better work visa. I contacted over ten lawyers, and none of them would take my case—they all said there was no way the government would give me the visa without having a degree.

Finally, I found a lawyer who would help me. We figured out a way to convince the government that my talent plus all my years of experience was equivalent to a degree.

I got the visa.

I had accomplished "Mission Impossible," I thought. After waiting for two years, finding loopholes, and sweet-talking my way through the process, I was finally going to film school. But as soon as I thought I had succeeded, I encountered my biggest obstacle.

Until that day, I hadn't actually walked around the UT Austin campus, so I didn't know it was one of the biggest campuses in the U.S. The day I realized how big it was, I was terrified. I didn't think I would be able to walk from class to class.

When I was young, I had two major injuries that have affected my life ever since. I was in a terrible car accident, and I had a really bad groin injury. Because I grew up poor, I didn't have the money to go to the doctor, and the injuries got worse over time. The car accident affected my neck and eventually my back; I started having pinched nerves in my back every couple of years. The groin injury affected the way I walk. To this day, I have to think about every single step I take. For a long time, I couldn't walk or stand for too long. I would get extremely tired. I couldn't see how I was going to walk across the UT Austin campus on a regular basis.

For the six months before classes started, I focused on getting strong and healthy. I turned a shed next to my trailer into a physical therapy room. I bought a weighted vest that could carry up to 40 pounds. Every single day, I did squats and went running while wearing that vest. At first I could only do a couple of squats, and run for less than a mile. Over time, though, I was doing dozens of squats and running for more than three miles.

Little by little, I could feel my body getting stronger, and I could walk farther and stand for a longer period of time. Sometimes I would scream so loudly while pushing myself that Martin could hear me all the way to his house, and he would come down to check on me.

The trailer was tiny, and I think that was what I loved the most about it. Everything inside was completely necessary. I was forced to have an extremely simple life. I think that simplicity was the main reason I was able to focus so much on my recovery.

When I think about the time I spent at the trailer, it feels like a flash—like a side story that happened in-between lives. I felt like I was in a cave away from others, finding out what I was capable of.

The first day of school came quickly. As I walked across campus, I couldn't contain my excitement. I was looking around to see if anyone would notice that I was walking just fine. But, of course, there's nothing extraordinary about a guy walking to class.

When I got to the door of my first class, I stopped. I was so nervous I was almost shaking. It took me years to get to that moment: just to go to a class, just so I could learn.

Finally, I had made it happen, and part of me couldn't believe it. Part of me felt like if I went inside the classroom, something would go wrong. I would realize it was too good to be true. Maybe the admissions office would notice that I didn't have the right type of visa, and someone would come and ask me to follow them.

So I waited at the door. I'm not sure what I was waiting for, but I waited. Everyone else was walking past me, taking their seats and looking at their phones, but I couldn't move. I called my friend Manny, hoping he would give me some kind of encouragement, but he didn't answer. I left a message on his phone. "I did it, I accomplished Mission Impossible!" I said to the machine, trying to convince myself it was real.

Finally, I mustered up the courage to walk inside the classroom. I sat down and waited for the professor to start the class, and nobody from the admissions office came for me.

At that moment, I thought about the woman in that office who told me there was no way I could go to UT Austin, and I felt thankful. I was grateful to her for telling me I couldn't do something, because she gave me no option but to show her I could.

And not only did I get in, but I received a scholarship that paid for the entire tuition!

I think a lot about those times in my life when I had to overcome a seemingly impossible obstacle, like leaving home, living with Winn, making a business, and going to film school. All those achievements and successes have something in common: I accepted my starting point.

Instead of wasting time and energy feeling bad because I couldn't walk, or because I didn't have the right visa, or because I didn't have the money, I just got to work. I earned it. I accepted that even though my starting point was so far away from my goals, it was still a starting point. And I realized that it didn't matter how far away I was, I could still do something about it.

Chapter
— Four —
Accepting the Consequences

Eight months before I was planning to graduate, a girl came to my class and made an announcement. "I'm part of a program that takes students around the world," she said. She explained that the program created content to promote non-profit organizations.

She described a program where students traveled all over the world, taking photographs, making videos, and sharing stories worth telling. I felt like someone had taken my dream from my head and made it a reality. Right away I signed up, and after a couple of interviews I got the role of main filmmaker. That was the closest I had ever been to my dream since I left home.

As soon as I got accepted, I realized that the student program was in the summer, and I was planning to graduate in the summer. By this time, I had already drilled into my head that nothing was going to come easy, so I wasn't surprised about the conflict.

I sat down and wrote an intricate plan with all the possible ways I could be a part of the student program *and* graduate at the same time. After hours of planning, I found the best option was to take 21 hours of credits the following semester. After that, I would only have to take one class during the summer, which was perfect.

I had to be an active student at UT Austin to be a part of the program, so I took a class called "Special Project" so that I could travel during the summer. The class consisted of making a project in your own time, and having a mentor along the way. I persuaded my mentor that my "Special Project" was traveling the world, taking photos and video for nonprofits. On top of that, I had to convince the school to let me take that many credits, which I did.

That was the semester I worked the hardest during my time at UT Austin. I spent every waking hour doing schoolwork. I even went on a super-strict raw vegetable diet, because I was sure that would help me focus.

Part of the plan was that because I was going to be so busy at school, I wouldn't have time to work. Because I was not going to have time to work, I would go broke. And because I was going to go broke, I would be homeless. So basically, my plan was to go broke and homeless so I could finish school and be a part of the program.

That was the best plan I had.

Once I realized what I needed to do to accomplish my goal, I sat down and took a deep breath. Then I asked myself, *Are you willing to go broke and homeless to pursue your dreams?* Without hesitation, my answer was yes. I was willing to sacrifice everything for my dreams, even if the consequences were going broke and becoming homeless.

The next semester, I devoted 16 hours a day to school, and gave up a lot of sleep and friends. I was extremely focused that entire semester. The main reason I was able to be so devoted to my dream was because I had already accepted the consequences beforehand. I had thought about the worst-case scenario, and as intimidating as it sounded, I was willing to endure it.

During my entire last semester at school, I kept pushing forward—no matter how hard it got. Because nothing got as bad as my worst-case scenario, the semester was just paperwork to me.

That summer, I successfully finished my last semester at school. I was now ready to go travel the world, doing what I loved. My team and I went to Mexico and China to do work for the Livestrong Foundation. Our job was to create documentaries that could help erase the stigma surrounding cancer in those countries; many people wrongly believe that "cancer is contagious," "cancer does not have a cure," or "cancer is a punishment from God." First we went to Mexico. Livestrong had created a campaign called "Comparte Tu Historia" ("Share your Story"), and they had a dozen or so cancer survivors sharing their stories of strength. They wanted to educate the audience about cancer, and our job was to document the effects of the campaign.

After Mexico, we went to China. Livestrong's goal was to create a similar campaign there, and our job was to document the stigmas that cancer had there. People in China were ashamed of having cancer, and some died alone because they didn't want to share the news with their loved ones.

That trip was one of the most fulfilling and emotional experiences I've ever had. Even though we only traveled for a month, that was the first time I got to live my dream. Traveling around the world, doing what I love, and helping people—it doesn't get much better than that.

On that trip I learned the power of storytelling, and I understood that capturing stories comes with a big responsibility. We got to interview cancer survivors and hear their perspective on cancer. Those people opened their lives, their homes, and their hearts to us. We became friends and even felt like family in a matter of hours. They shared with us their deepest sorrows and their greatest hopes. We listened to them talk about death and pain, and life and joy. They talked to us as if we were very old friends. They showed me what true vulnerability is, and they taught me that vulnerability breaks barriers.

It was then I realized that some people just need to be heard. Some people just need to share their story. Talking to one of the cancer survivors, I asked why she was so willing to talk about her disease. She said she knew other people with cancer would hear her story, and that it would help them find strength and feel less lonely. She felt it was her duty to help them. When she told me that, I understood that my responsibility was to share her story in the most honest, raw, compassionate way I could.

When we came back home, we spent the next month editing the project, and it was a great success. But it came at a really big price, because we had to work extremely hard to get it done. I had to be completely engaged physically, mentally, and emotionally. Going back to the interviews made me very emotional; I think I cried just about every day. Trying to do justice to the cancer survivors' stories brought a lot of stress.

Just before we finished the project, I had to have gallbladder surgery. I guess I had pushed myself too hard for too long without taking care of myself. Around the same time, I got a pinched nerve in my back, which left me barely able to walk.

I had been getting these pinched nerves every couple of years for the previous six years. I expected to be broke and homeless, but I never thought that on top of that I would have surgery, a back injury, and be emotionally drained. But if you had asked me at the time if it was worth it, I would have answered, "Absolutely!" I literally gave everything I had to that project, and there is no bigger sense of fulfillment that comes from that.

Looking back at that time in my life makes me realize that when we accept the consequences of our goals, anything is possible. I think one of the main reasons we don't accomplish what we want is because we don't know what we're willing to do for it. Once we know the sacrifices and accept the consequences, then it's only about moving forward.

Chapter
— Five —
One Step at a Time

After I finished the project for Livestrong, I was broke, homeless, recuperating from gallbladder surgery, and had a pinched nerve in my back. I ended up staying with a girl I was dating—which, by the way, I messed up big time. But that's a story for another time.

I was exhausted. I had pushed myself till I was completely drained. It was hard to focus, and I felt physically defeated. The pinched nerve in my back was barely letting me walk. My abdomen hurt because of the surgery, and my overall energy was down. I think life sometimes lets us know when it's time for a change, and that's how I felt. I saw everything I was going through as a message for me to make a big change in my life. I saw it as an opportunity to reinvent myself, and that's what I did.

I told myself I needed time to heal mentally, physically, emotionally, and spiritually. I told myself I needed to be away for a while, away from anything and anyone I knew. So an idea started forming in my mind. More than an idea, I guess it was just a simple thought:

Be nothing, so you can become everything.

At first, I didn't know how to interpret that thought. For a while it didn't make any sense or have any meaning. But as the thought kept coming into my mind, I began to realize what it meant, or at least what I thought it meant.

Since I was a kid, I have always dreamt that at some point in my life I would become a great man—a man who other men would want to be like, a man who women would want to be with. I wanted to be a man with an unbendable code of honor, who is driven by compassion. At that moment, to be honest, I was extremely far from being that man.

For me to become everything I always wanted to be, I decided I first needed to get rid of everything I was. I needed to become new again. I needed to get rid of all the roles I was playing in my life. I needed to be nothing, have nothing, need nothing. Once I could do that, I thought, I could truly be myself—I could become everything I always wanted to be.

For a while, I thought about going to Canada or South America. But one day I remembered a book by Shirley MacLaine, where she talks about her experience walking the famous pilgrimage Camino de Santiago in Spain.

The pilgrimage entails walking the entire country of Spain from border to sea—almost 40 days of walking, 500 miles total, with an average of 17 miles per day. (I didn't pay too much attention to those details at the time.) As soon as I thought about that book, I knew I needed to go to Spain. Now, I don't know why I thought walking across Spain would heal me mentally, physically, emotionally, and spiritually, but I did. And I don't know why I thought I would be able to walk across Spain, since I could barely walk at the time, but I did. And I have no idea why I thought walking across Spain would help me become nothing so I could become everything, but I did.

Without any doubt or hesitation, I sold everything I had, including the old white

Pathfinder that I bartered with Martin. I also gave away most of my clothes. While I was getting ready for the trip, I saw a homeless man walking on the street. I asked him if he wanted some clothes. He never expected a full trash bag! It felt good to give everything away. It felt good to give my clothes to someone who needed it more than I did.

Not too long after that, I flew to Spain. I arrived in Madrid, took a train to Pamplona, then took a cab across the border to France. I arrived in a small town called St Jean Pied de Port, where I started my pilgrimage.

If I wanted to stay in one of the shelters along the route, or get a diploma at the end, I needed a pilgrim's passport. As soon as I arrived in town, I went straight to the pilgrim's office to get my passport, then to the town's shelter to get ready for my first day of walking.

The place was full of people from all over the world. They were either resting from the day's walk or, like me, just starting their journey. The pilgrimage attracted really specific type of people. It seemed that just like me, everyone who was there was going through some type of transition: some had just graduated from college, some had gotten divorced or quit their jobs, and some just wanted to find what was next for them in their life. Every person I met was excited and open to the idea of creating a new life through that pilgrimage. I was just excited to be able to walk.

I settled in to my room at the shelter, and spread out all my things on the floor. Since I was supposed to walk across an entire country, I wanted to make sure I wasn't carrying anything that wasn't absolutely necessary. When I packed everything inside my backpack, it weighed around 40 pounds. It reminded me of the vest I used to wear while training, so I could walk across UT Austin.

Once I finished packing, I looked at the schedule for the first day—and was shocked. I got so excited getting ready for the trip, selling my car, and giving away my clothes, that I kind of forgot to research how many miles a day I was supposed to walk. The next morning, I was supposed to walk across the Pyrenees, one of the greatest mountain ranges in the world. I flipped through the schedule and my jaw dropped to the ground. I had to walk an average of 17 miles every single day for the next 40 days. From border to sea, I was supposed to walk the entire country of Spain.

A couple of weeks before, I couldn't even walk, and the next day I was supposed to walk 17 miles across the Pyrenees. *I sure know how to get myself into interesting situations,* I thought. Instead of focusing on how big the obstacle seemed, I tried to concentrate on the fact that I was about to start the biggest adventure of my life. I went to bed excited and nervous at the same time.

The next morning I woke up early, got ready, put the 40-pound backpack on, and started walking. After hours of walking, we got to the top of our first mountain, and the view was breathtaking. From horizon to horizon you could only see green mountaintops. It felt like I hadn't actually smelled fresh air before. It was so peaceful, majestic, and powerful. I remember telling a fellow pilgrim that I couldn't believe that just a couple of weeks before I was broke, homeless, recuperating from a surgery, and had a pinched nerve in my back—and here I was, climbing the Pyrenees. I felt a deep sense of accomplishment.

But as the hours passed by, I started to realize that my body was not ready for this journey. My knees and back were too weak to walk at that pace for the next couple of weeks. Every single step I took made me realize that my body and my mind were not strong enough. But at the same time, I knew my spirit was, so I kept moving forward.

As I walked that first day, I started to feel pressure in my knees, and for a while I wondered whether I could finish the pilgrimage. Deep inside I knew the answer was yes, because there was no Option B. I had just left everything, once again, to seek for a transformation in my life, and physical and mental pain were not going to stop me.

I was still committed to the thought of becoming nothing so I could become everything, and at that point it was clear that I was in the "becoming nothing" part. I was shedding away my pain and my doubt. For the first time in a long time, I was focused on being nothing but who I was *at the moment*. Being with myself, by myself, was something I hadn't done in a long time.

As I kept walking, though, the pressure in my knees kept building. After 10 hours of hiking, I finally got to the finish line for the day. By the time I settled down in the shelter, I was wiped out. I had never before hiked 17 miles in one day, and I couldn't see myself doing it again the next day. My knees were so sore that I wondered if I could even stand the next day.

I fell asleep just after dinner. When I woke up, I could barely open my eyes. I felt like I had never in my life been that tired. Without thinking too much more about it, I stood up, put the 40-pound backpack on, and started walking again.

As soon as I took the first step, I felt pressure on my knees; it hadn't gone away during the night. With every single step, the pressure kept building. The pain combined with my exhaustion made the second day a constant struggle.

After a couple of hours, the pressure in my knees built up so much that I started wondering if I would be able to finish the pilgrimage. *How am I going to endure this for the next 40 days?* I asked myself. For the next couple of hours, every single step I took got a little bit more painful than the one before. One step, pain. Another step, more pain. One more step, even more pain. It got to the point where I was scared to take the next step.

I started to feel bad not only because of the pain, but because I saw that I was one of the slower pilgrims. It made me mad to see that no one seemed to be struggling nearly as much as I was. It was just a reminder that there was something wrong with me, that I had an injury. It was a reminder that I was weak.

Eight hours after I started walking on that painful second day, I finally got to the shelter. Again I crashed as soon as I finished dinner, and when I woke up, I could barely open my eyes due to the exhaustion. *I can't believe I have to do this one more time,* I said to myself. *What did I get myself into??* I forced myself to stop thinking about it and put the 40-pound backpack on. As soon as I took the first step, I felt pain in my knees.

The day before, I'd had to deal with intense pain for the last couple of hours. This day, it seemed that I would have to endure pain the entire ten hours of walking. That thought devastated me.

After a couple of hours of walking really slowly, the pain turned very sharp. I knew my pilgrimage was over—there was no way I could continue that misery for the next couple of weeks.

My focus turned from trying to finish the pilgrimage, to trying to finish the day. As the sharp pain kept building, I felt more and like a failure. When I finally got to the destination, I was demoralized. I had already decided that would be the last day of my journey. I felt weak, broken, and beaten-down. I was not as strong as I'd hoped I would be.

I settled in, discouraged. A moment later, another pilgrim approached me.

"I've been watching you all day, and I've noticed you've been struggling," he said kindly. "I have some 1000mg ibuprofen pills. Take one; it'll help." I had no idea there were 1000mg pills of anything! I gladly took the pill.

Just as he left, another pilgrim came up to me.

"Hey, I have this cream I use every time I hike a lot," he said, offering me a tube. "Try it. It's going to help your knees." Without hesitation, I rubbed the cream on my knees.

A couple of minutes later, a third pilgrim came over to me with a bag of ice. At that point I didn't care what it was—I wanted to try it all. I put the ice on my knee. A minute later, a woman approached me.

"Do you believe I can heal you with my hands?" she asked. *Why not?* I thought. She kneeled down, hovered her hands on top of my knees, and started whispering something.

By the end of the night, I had tried all the remedies the other pilgrims had offered. My knees didn't immediately feel better, but *I* felt better. I thought about my situation and decided I would try walking one more time, after resting for a day. The small possibility of continuing gave me hope.

The next day I woke up, put my feet on the floor, stood up, and realized that my knees didn't hurt. There was pressure, but not pain. I took one step and I felt fine. A second step and no pain. I did a squat, and still nothing. *I can totally do this*, I thought to myself. *You can walk another 17 miles today!*

Before I set out that day, I came up with a plan. I told myself that during the entire day I would only focus on *my* progress. No more focusing on the pilgrim going ahead of me, going faster than me. The same with the person behind me—I would not pay attention to the pilgrim going slower than me. No focusing on the pilgrim next to me, either. I would not compare myself to anyone that day.

Today you're only going to focus on yourself, your path, your goal, and taking one step at a time, I said to myself.

Every time I wanted to see how another pilgrim was doing, I would look down and focus only on my own path. Then I would look up and see my final destination, my goal. I would focus on taking one step, then the next one, and then another one.

I also told myself that whenever I couldn't walk any longer, I would take a break for as long as necessary. Then I would stand back up and continue walking until I couldn't walk any more. I would repeat that process till I got to my goal. Walk, rest. Walk, rest.

After I had given myself this pep talk, I put on the 40-pound backpack and started walking. My entire focus was on every single step. Right away, the other pilgrims left me behind, but I reminded myself that I would only focus on *my* journey that day.

A couple of hours into the day, I started feeling pain. As soon as I did, I sat down and took a break. When I was ready, I stood back up and started walking once again. I kept doing this over and over again. Before I knew it, I had walked 14 miles! It's amazing how far we can go when we focus on going at our own pace.

Towards the end of the day, I finally looked up and saw a massive mountain right in front of me. With all the commotion the night before, I had forgotten to look at the schedule—so I didn't realize that at the end of the day I was supposed to climb a huge mountain. I stood there looking at it for what seemed like an eternity.

"Well, I'm already here," I said out loud. After taking a really deep breath, I continued walking.

For the next couple of hours, I tried to not focus on the size of the enormous obstacle I needed to overcome. Instead, once again I focused on taking one small step at time. As I walked up the path, the mountain got steeper and steeper. The steeper it got, the more pain I felt. When I couldn't take it anymore, I would take a break, then get back up when I was ready.

I followed my plan for the next couple of hours, and finally I reached the top of the mountain. There have only been a few times in my life when I felt as proud as I did that moment. I couldn't even recall any of the other times right then, perhaps because no other accomplishment has taken so much grit and determination.

As soon as I dropped my backpack on the ground, a powerful sense of achievement overcame me. I was extremely pleased with what I had done that day. My plan was to take a break for the rest of the day and continue the journey the following morning. Even though I was only miles away from the finish line, I thought I had pushed myself too hard already.

I sat down to admire the view. In the distance, I could see beautiful mountains and valleys. I could also see a tiny town not too far ahead from me—the destination for that day's journey. I could see the finish line, and it didn't look far at all. Even though it was getting late, I couldn't stop that close to my goal.

I stood back up and told myself, *I can totally do this. I can get there.* I started walking down the mountain. As soon as I took the first step going down, I knew it was going to be way harder on my knees than going up. That first step was very painful. The next couple of steps were extremely painful. By the time I had walked a couple hundred feet, I was feeling more pain than I'd ever felt before.

I stopped. With my head down, I could feel tears running down my cheeks. My tears were not because of the pain—I cried because I was so tired of feeling broken. I was so tired of feeling that I was not enough, that there was something wrong with me. I was so tired of feeling that I would never amount to anything great because I was too weak.

As the tears kept running down my face, I started to take deep breaths. Then I said to myself, almost involuntarily, *I'm not weak. I'm not weak. I'm not weak. I'm not weak.* That calmed me down. Suddenly, the words "I'm strong" came out of my mouth. That was extremely powerful.

For the next couple of minutes, I kept telling myself that I was strong over and over again. Eventually, I started yelling, "I'm strong! I'm strong! I'm strong!" I lifted my head up and took one step. As soon as my foot touched the ground I felt the sharp pain in my knee, but I did not stop.

I felt pain with every step I took, but as soon as I did, I would yell, "I'm strong!" at the top of my lungs. The pain kept getting stronger, but so did I. Tears were coming out uncontrollably, but I kept focusing on taking one step at a time, and telling myself I was strong. And for that moment, I was.

Before I knew it, I was almost to the bottom of the mountain. At that point, I started bawling. There has only been one other time in my life when I sobbed that much—when I was seven, and I had just found out that my cousins had invited my brothers to their house, but not me. This sobbing was different, though. It wasn't the pain, and it wasn't because I was tired of feeling weak. I was crying because I was thankful to God for giving me the strength to keep moving forward. This time

I was crying because I felt strong, and that was a new feeling for me.

When I got to the bottom of the mountain, I felt extremely grateful. It felt like I had not only conquered a massive mountain, but myself as well. A couple of hours later, I achieved my goal for the day, and the dinner and rest that night were the best during my entire journey.

For the rest of the pilgrimage, I never again wondered if I would be able to finish it. After my experience on the mountain, every single day I kept getting stronger. It wasn't long before I had already walked the entire country of Spain.

Only two weeks before I started my pilgrimage, I could barely walk. Forty days later, I had walked 500 miles, from the French border to the Atlantic Ocean.

Chapter
– Six –
Love Yourself For Who You Are

Some people believe that The Camino does not end when you arrive in Santiago de Compostela, but it follows you home instead. The true journey begins when you go back home, as someone new, to your old life. The true challenge comes in applying everything you learned during the pilgrimage to your regular life.

Because of that, people take some time before going back home. It's an abrupt change to go from walking across mountains every day to being stuck in traffic for hours at a time. Some who go back home as soon as they finish The Camino can experience depression—normal life is just not as inspiring as a pilgrimage. Other people take months to get back home; they travel around for a while and slowly settle back into regular life. That's what I did.

When I finished the pilgrimage there was a part of me that wasn't ready to go back home. It felt like the Camino had helped release the old me—it helped me get rid of anger, self-doubt, and grudges against other people and myself. It helped me forgive many things others had done to me, and many that I had done to others. I felt lighter than I had in years. I felt acceptance toward others, but mainly toward myself—and that was something I hadn't felt before.

I felt new. For the first time, I understood what Christ meant when he said you couldn't put new wine into old wineskin, because it would burst. The old me was full of doubt, fear, and grudges. Now that I was empty, it was time to fill myself up with new wine—love, compassion, and understanding, especially toward myself.

That trip was the starting point of learning to love myself. Before my journey, I couldn't remember the last time I had truly taken care of myself. I couldn't remember the last time I had loved myself. I thought I had a great opportunity to do that while I was away from home, so instead of going back to the U.S., I decided to travel around Europe.

First I spent some time traveling around Spain. I went to Madrid, Barcelona, and finally Malaga in southern Spain. A girl I met while walking on The Camino invited me to spend a week with her.

Then I flew to Ireland to see another friend I met during the pilgrimage. She lived in a tiny town south of Dublin. Ireland is one of the most beautiful countries I've ever been to—when you look at the horizon, you can see dozens of shades of green on the mountains.

From there I took a ferry to Wales. Jonathan, another friend from the pilgrimage, invited me to stay with him and his family in a small town. He lives in a cabin in the mountains, and I stayed in an attic room for a couple of months.

Those two months were by far the best investment in myself that I have made in my entire life. My only focus during that time was to get to know and love myself.

One day, I called my mom to let her know I was fine, but that she wouldn't be hearing from me for a while.

"What do you mean?" she asked.

"Well... for a while I don't want to be anything else but me," I explained. "I don't want to be a son, a brother, a boyfriend, a photographer, or anything else."

She was quiet. Most of the time my mom thinks I'm crazy. This was one of those times.

It sounded crazy, I agree, but to me it made perfect sense. How was I supposed to be a good son, brother, boyfriend, or photographer if I didn't take care of and love myself first?

So for the next couple of months, I lived in a cabin in Wales. It was exciting to be in a place where nobody knew anything about me. It was exhilarating to be in a cabin in the middle of the mountains with no distractions—it forced me to focus on myself. For those two months, I got to know who I was. I got to enjoy my own company. I got to dream about my future again.

Every single day, I would go for a walk in the forest. I had no goal or objective; the point was simply to relearn how to wonder and be curious, and how to feel admiration again. I followed the same path every day, and each time I would find something new. It made me wonder if that new thing was there the day before, or if I was just more aware that day.

As the days passed by, I felt like I was getting to know the forest. It reminded me of when I was a kid, spending hours by myself in the mountains in front of my house. It was there I learned that feeling lonely and being alone are two completely different things. I never felt lonely during my walks in that forest in Wales, even though I was alone.

Those walks would last for hours. Sometimes I would sit down and meditate; sometimes I would pray. And as I started to become more aware of my environment, I started to become more aware of my own self. I was constantly aware of how I felt.

I realized that for a long time I had focused on trying to make *other* people happy. I had focused on other people's feelings, and had forgotten about mine. The time and space that I created for myself to wonder gave me the time and space to listen to what was inside.

A sense of belonging started to take over me—a sense of peace and constant joy. It's kind of funny to realize that I felt the most satisfaction when I wasn't working toward a goal.

There have only been a few times in my life when I felt I was in the right place at the right time. One of those times was in Wales. I was reading inside the cabin, sitting next to the window, and I closed my book to admire the mountains. For a second I was speechless—the beauty just overwhelmed me. Then I noticed how *present* I felt, and I realized that it had been a long time since I had felt so content with the present moment. Then I knew that I was supposed to be there, at the cabin in Wales, at that exact moment.

Later in life, I would learn that being in the right place at the right time has a lot more to do with awareness than with timing and placement.

Letting myself *be* was something really fun to do. It felt like I was experimenting. I wondered whether life was about having experiences more than finding some really deep meaning. I wondered if life was just about living how you wanted to live—like being in a big old playground with a lot of games to play. I wondered if I had chosen the right games to play so far, and decided the answer was probably no. But it didn't really matter, because I could always choose another game to play, at any moment.

For example, I learned that I love to chop wood. I mean, I LOVE to chop wood. Almost every day, I would go to the back of the house to get some logs to fire up the stove. Those small logs had to be chopped in smaller pieces so they would fit. Chopping wood became a ritual, and that hour was probably the most fulfilling time of my entire day.

I would put my headphones on and play the soundtrack of *The Assassination of Jesse James*. Then I would focus my entire attention on each stroke, making sure I was using the right technique and the right amount of force. Chopping wood was my meditation practice.

During my breaks, I would admire the landscape. One time, I was staring at the clouds when I suddenly felt tears welling up in my eyes. Now, it's not like I cry all the time—I'm just recounting some of the most intense experiences of my life.

As I felt the tears falling down my cheeks, I also felt deep gratitude for my father—God, my creator. He was always there guiding me to that moment, chopping wood in a cabin in the middle of the mountains in Wales, when I discovered who I really was. I was grateful that God taught me how to *be* myself and *love* myself again.

That night, I wrote this down in a notebook:

More than a decade ago, on a full moon night, a kid sat by his window contemplating a beautiful rock. He started to talk to the moon about his dreams and how he wished that one day he could shine as much as she did. After saying that, he paused for a moment.

"I apologize, I don't want to shine like you do," he said to the moon. "You only reflect light from the Sun. I wish that one day I could be the source of light, and shine as bright as a star."

After almost 20 years, that wish is still as strong as it was that night.

Early in life, a huge urge for exploration and growth started to absorb me. My spirit encouraged me to travel and learn about other cultures; to push myself physically, and to expand and grow spiritually.

At the same time, a quieter voice was saying something else: that the only purpose for me to grow was to improve the lives of others. I knew I could share faith and wisdom. I could make people smile. I could inspire people to follow their dreams and their inner voice.

I have given up money, love, family, and friends to follow my spirit. I have endured loneliness and physical and emotional pain. I have made a lot of mistakes, but

I've learned from them—some the easy way, and some the hard way. I have hurt people and people have hurt me.

But all that was not enough. Some months ago, my inner voice started to talk to me again, and said that I had not given everything up yet. It told me I had to be nothing so I could become everything. It told me that if I wanted to become a better man, I needed to give my entire life to others. Then—and only then—could I truly know myself. Only then could I truly reach people. So I did—I sold the few things I owned and gave away most of my clothes to set out on a pilgrimage.

If you are one of those people who have been touched somehow by my work or my life, please know that I have done my best. Please know that my life's purpose is to inspire you. Everything has been worth it, just for you. Know that there is someone who has risked everything just so you could have a better day—even if it's just by sharing how I see the world.

I believed I could become a better man by helping people see the world differently. And thanks to that, I think I shine a little brighter today. Thanks to that, I feel a little bit closer to God.

*

During those two months in Wales, I focused on getting as fit as I could. Jonathan had a separate cabin that I used as my training room. Before dinner each night, I did one of those Insanity workouts. If you haven't done one, let me tell you they are truly insane.

At some point, my goal became more than just getting stronger—I was trying to fight the cold, too. It was January in the mountains of Wales, and it got pretty chilly. By the end of those two months, I was stronger physically than I had ever been before.

As my time in Wales was coming to an end, I started to feel that I was ready to move on, to go back home. The day before I left there was a massive snowstorm, and it felt like it was my graduation celebration. I went outside and did snow angels, then went for my last walk. I'll never forget it.

The place I had gotten to know so closely—the forest where I had spent so many hours—looked like a completely different place. It was a side of the forest I had never seen, but it was just as beautiful as the other side I had known. That day I learned how to admire the world for what it is. It made me wonder, how could I love one side more than the other? How could one side be more special than the other? The truth is that both sides of the forest are special, beautiful, and breathtaking.

That day I remembered that everything follows a natural process, which is no less than magical, sublime, and perfect. It's a process that is forever evolving.

I learned to not judge nature or myself through my understanding of things. I learned to see nature and myself with full openness and admiration, with no filter, with a quiet mind. Only then can I truly love nature . . . and myself.

The next day I left Wales. I left the place that helped me remember how to love myself for who I was. And I will forever be grateful.

Chapter Seven
STRENGTHS, NOT WEAKNESSES

JUST BEFORE BUYING MY PLANE TICKET HOME, I saw the movie *Brave*, a Disney animation film set in Scotland. I fell in love with the Celtic culture. As luck would have it, I found out there would be a Celtic music festival in Scotland the week of my birthday. So at the last minute, I canceled my plans to celebrate the big day on a road trip from California to Texas, and flew to Scotland instead.

The festival was fascinating, just as Scottish people are. I met up with a couple of friends from the pilgrimage, and then we took a road trip through the lake region. A week later I flew to England, and from there I finally flew back home.

By the time I came back to Texas, I felt whole. I was in great shape physically. My mind was calm. I felt a constant sense of thankfulness, and I felt at peace with God. It turned out I was right—that journey was just what I needed to heal.

It wasn't just the pilgrimage in Spain that healed me, though—it was also my time in that cabin in Wales, and my travels around Europe, that helped me be whole again. It was the time and space I gave myself to focus all my intention on myself, listening to what was within. I had a presence and confidence that I hadn't before.

As soon as I got back home, a friend from UT Austin film school invited me to be part of a project called "Pedal South." Jack told me the plan was to cycle 14,000 miles from Alaska to Argentina over the course of 21 months. We would be making a documentary along the way, and I would be one of the filmmakers.

When Jack invited me I was still in Wales, and at the time I wasn't sure if I wanted to be a part of it. One thing I understood about myself during my time in Europe was that I didn't want to travel just for the sake of traveling anymore. I learned that what fulfills me is traveling to give others a perspective of what is out there in the world.

After thinking about it, I realized that Pedal South was the perfect project to do that. Traveling down the length of the Americas would give me the opportunity to share stories of the people and cultures along the way.

I also decided that if my goal was to share knowledge and wisdom, to serve people, then now would be the perfect time to do it. I had never been so centered, so strong, and so present, and I needed to be in that state to be able to help others.

The following months passed very quickly. I started from scratch when I returned from Europe, so I was busy finding a new place to live and adjusting to a new routine. I also began working as a director of photography for movies. Between all that and doing pre-production on the trip, life seemed to move faster than normal. Pretty soon we were only six months away from flying to Alaska.

One day, out of the blue, I got another pinched nerve in my back. This time was different, though; I had never experienced that amount of pain before, not even when I was walking across Spain. It was so painful I couldn't walk for a couple of weeks, and I couldn't sleep. That injury broke me completely—physically, mentally, and emotionally. It literally felt like it broke my heart and my spirit.

I know a pinched nerve may not sound like a big deal, but it is. It happens when a nerve in your spinal cord gets pressed between bone and ligament, and it causes horrible pain to go all the way up to your neck and down to your feet. The pain is almost constant.

For years, a pinched nerve was my Achilles' heel. I thought I had done everything I needed to do to get better. I sold everything I owned, gave away my clothes, walked Spain, and spent months in the mountains of Wales. None of my sacrifices had made any difference.

"Becoming nothing so I could become everything" had made no difference. In fact, I was in a worse place than where I had been before. For the first time in my life, I felt completely hopeless.

That was the hardest and the darkest period of my life. Even today, it's hard to believe I was able to stand back up after feeling so discouraged and broken.

For the following months, I felt lost, alone, and a failure. I kept telling myself that I was broken and weak. My entire focus was on being depressed. Knowing we were only months away from leaving to Alaska overwhelmed me—I couldn't see how I was going to recover from this, much less be ready to cycle down the Americas. All I could focus on was this massive obstacle.

In the past, every time I had to overcome a big problem, I knew I had the energy to do it. I knew I had the faith and could find the way. But this time, I didn't have any of that. I couldn't see a way out.

It got so bad that I ended up calling my mom. That was the first time since I left home that I had asked for her help. She knows me better than anybody else, and I knew she could help me. Without hesitation, she flew from Mexico to come live with me in Texas for a couple of months.

As soon as she arrived, she saw the bad shape I was in. She said I looked like I had given up, and she had never seen me like that before. That was exactly how I felt: knocked down. I just lay on the ground and could not find a way to get back up.

Days passed by and nothing really changed. Slowly the pain started to go away, but it didn't really matter, because I was still mentally broken. I was so overwhelmed and discouraged to think that all my time on the pilgrimage and in Wales had been for nothing.

One day, my mom had had enough of my feeling sorry for myself. She said to me, "Ricardo, my son is not a coward. So you're not going to tell me that fucking back pain is going to break you down!"

There's not much you can say to something like that.

My mom has always had a unique way of teaching me things. As soon as I heard her say that, something clicked. I realized that I had been spending months focusing on my weaknesses and obstacles. I began to turn my attention to my strengths, my goals, and my desired outcome.

I started to focus not on how weak I was, but on how strong I could be. Not on how lost I felt, but on how much purpose I could have. I began focusing on creating a way—not on how I had lost my way.

I realized that the more I focused on being weak, the weaker I was, but the more I focused on being strong, the stronger I became. I learned that this idea applies to everything. If I focused on being sad, I would become sadder; if I focused on being happy, I would become happier.

So I reminded myself that I still had a dream of traveling around the world, and that Pedal South was a vehicle for me to touch the lives of people across the Americas. If I didn't get better, I couldn't help those people. This journey was about something much bigger than me: it was about serving others through doing what I love.

I started focusing on the outcome, not on my obstacles, and that's what got me out of my depression—knowing that I had the potential to improve the life of others, and if I did not get better, that opportunity would be wasted.

I started imagining myself cycling down the Americas. I imagined myself sharing stories and crossing the finish line at the bottom of the world.

Months passed by, and slowly, step by step, I got stronger physically. More importantly, I got stronger mentally—the negative thoughts were not appearing in my mind as often. I had a purpose again.

My family started getting really concerned about me. They thought my body was not going to be strong enough to cycle down two continents, that at some point during the trip my back would give out. They reminded me that not too long before, I couldn't even walk. But I didn't pay any attention. I remembered that I had hiked across an entire country, when just weeks before that I could barely walk.

I kept my focus on getting strong and achieving my goal. I put all my attention toward my desired outcome.

Those months of darkness taught me something really important: sometimes brokenness is necessary. Sometimes we need to experience complete hopelessness, because only then do we have the opportunity to realize how strong we can be.

I also learned that I was wrong for believing that I needed to be strong before I could share wisdom and knowledge. When I came back from Europe, I was strong, centered, and balanced, but I finally understood that that's not the ideal state to be in if you want to help people. I realized that first I had to experience being completely broken, because that's what gave me perspective.

Being broken physically, mentally, and emotionally gave me compassion for others. I realized that everyone at some point in his or her life will go through some experience of being broken. The best way to connect with people is through vulnerability—we bond by sharing not only our hopes, but also our weaknesses.

Years before, I had asked God to help me become a great man. Being broken got me a little bit closer to that. I never thought that battling my darkest days would become the fastest path to grow as a man, but it was.

The truth is that now I understand that I asked for that. I wanted the opportunity to prove to myself that I could be even stronger. I asked to be able to connect with and serve people from all around the world. And God gave me that opportunity, even though I didn't recognize it at the time. I didn't see it, because it came in the form of a broken spirit.

Chapter
— *Eight* —
Learn to Love the Pain

On June 11, 2014, the Pedal South team was finally ready. We embarked on the greatest journey of our lives, and what had once seemed impossible turned into reality.

At the airport in Austin, family members and friends helped us carry in all our gear. Some were saying goodbye and wishing us well. Some were crying, and some looked really concerned. The only thing they had in common was that they all looked proud of us—and they all seemed a bit in awe, too.

During most of pre-production, a lot of people didn't think we were actually going to make the journey. I think at times even we ourselves had doubts. The day we left, we proved a lot of skeptics wrong—and to be honest, I think we proved something to ourselves as well.

I remember two things about that day: one, kissing my girlfriend goodbye, and two, taking a picture of the whole team inside the plane, wearing the Pedal South uniform.

We flew to Seattle, then to Fairbanks, and finally to Deadhorse, Alaska, the top of the world. It's right on the Arctic Ocean, pretty close to the North Pole. As we were getting off the airplane, the first thing that came out of my mouth was, "Did we just fuck up?!" It was so foggy that the only thing we could see was the tiny airport in front of the airplane, which looked more like a small motel.

At the baggage claim area—which was no bigger than a small apartment—we unboxed our bicycles and put them together. As we were filling the saddlebags with our gear, we noticed that the fuel for the stove was missing from one of our checked bags. We found out later that airport security had confiscated it. For a while, during our journey down the Americas, the FBI was looking for my friend who had innocently tried to transport it.

Without fuel, we couldn't cook the mountains of ramen we had brought. Luckily, there was a small store in Deadhorse—the only one in 500 miles—so we got what we thought was enough fuel for two weeks. We were also prepared with ingredients for PB&J sandwiches.

To officially start our trip, we took our bicycles to the northern edge of the world and dunked them into the Arctic Ocean. Then we started cycling south, which we would do for the next 21 months.

During the first stretch of the trip, we rode down the Dalton highway, a 500-mile gravel road that goes from the Arctic Ocean to Fairbanks, in the center of Alaska. In those 500 miles there are no stores, buildings, or people. Once in a while we saw a truck pass by.

For the next couple of days, I felt like I was in a really long dream. We were in Alaska in the summer, so we had 24 hours of sunlight. The sun doesn't set for weeks. It looks like it's 2 pm all the time, which felt like forever.

We cycled eight to ten hours a day, and the sun only moved from side to side across the sky. We would set up camp and have dinner, and the sun would still be high up. When we woke up, the sun would still look the same as it had the day before.

Every night I would get to camp completely exhausted. Before the trip, I had never cycled more than four hours straight, and here I was cycling an average of 10 hours a day, every day. I was taking 1000 mg of ibuprofen a day so I could endure the pain in my knees. Once again, I had set out to do something I wasn't ready for.

After just a week, we ran out of cooking fuel—we had made the wrong calculations for how much we needed. We were in the middle of Nowhere, Alaska. I kept thinking how just a week before, I had been living in a city, sleeping in a bed, working out maybe an hour a day, and eating plenty of food. Now here I was sleeping in a tent in the middle of Alaska, cycling 10-hour days, and surviving on dry ramen and two PB&J sandwiches a day.

We were hangry: constantly hungry and angry. Because the sun never set, it felt like a really long nightmare.

On top of that, we always had to be on the lookout for wildlife. In that part of the world you can encounter polar, black, and grizzly bears. Once in a while, a driver would stop to warn us that a grizzly bear was a mile ahead. There's only so much

I can take mentally, and that was getting pretty close to my threshold.

After a couple of days like this, suddenly in the distance we saw a sign that read "Happy Valley Camp." We looked off to the left of the road, and down the hill we could see a building. We rushed down and happily saw that it was a small dining area for the camp. In the back we could see the kitchen, and that's where we met Marcy.

The camp was for people who were working to clean up an oil leak nearby, and Marcy was the chef in charge of feeding everyone in the camp. I have never seen kinder eyes in my life, or such a beautiful smile. A powerful light was shining from within her, and she seemed truly at peace.

She could tell we were starving, and she took care of us like a mother would. There was something so familiar about how she made sure we were fed and comfortable.

Marcy gave us food and something to drink. She then told us her life story, which was fascinating. She's one of those rare people who have managed to always be doing what they want to be doing—one of those people who see life as an adventure, like a place where you come to play. She is one of the few who know how to truly enjoy the journey.

At one point she was a musher, driving dogsleds in competitions. Another time she was dropped in some deserted area of Alaska with a tent, food, and a shotgun to protect her from grizzly bears. I'm not sure what her job was there. The day we met her she was a chef, and she loved it as much as she had loved any of her other jobs. For now, she said, this was exactly what she wanted to do.

Marcy looked truly happy and content with what she was doing at that exact moment. I hadn't met too many people—myself included—who look content and joyful with their lives *right now*. I had always felt that happiness is just a step ahead—like I can't seem to get a hold on it. Because I'd always been extremely ambitious, I felt like I was constantly chasing happiness, and that caused a lot of dissatisfaction. I always thought that once I accomplished something, I'd be happy.

After dinner and a pleasant conversation, we went outside to set up camp. I couldn't get Marcy out of my head—her glow really stood out to me. I felt like I needed to ask for her advice.

I told her I had a big problem called "discontentment," and that it seemed she had figured out the solution. I told her that I wanted to do many things in my life, like she had, but I could never seem to find happiness in everyday life.

"Could you tell me how to stop being dissatisfied?" I asked. She looked at me with those beautiful eyes and smiled.

"You need to learn to love the pain," she said. "You need to learn to love the ugly. You need to learn to love the pain because that's where your love is needed the most."

No one has ever given me such profound advice. It helped me realize that happiness is not a goal you chase, but something you choose to experience. I started to think that maybe if we choose to love our pain, our struggles, and our obstacles, then we won't have to pursue happiness—it will just naturally come to us.

For the next 21 months, that's what I did. While I cycled down the Americas, I asked myself whether I could love being hungry, tired, and cold, whether I could love my doubt, fear, and pain. And the answer was always yes.

Every time I felt I was going to have a mental breakdown, every time we got robbed or slept in the dirt, every time I felt that I couldn't take it anymore, I thought about what Marcy said: "Learn to love the pain, because that's where your love is needed the most."

I forced myself to love those moments, because the potential for growth, change, and compassion is found within pain. The potential for self-discovery is also found in pain, and knowing yourself and conquering yourself is the biggest battle you will face in your life.

During those 21 months, pain helped me become a better man, because I learned where my love was needed the most.

Pedal South pushed me beyond what I thought was possible. I have tried to remember who I was before our journey, but I can't. It feels like the Ricardo that left never came back; instead, *I* came back—the new Ricardo. There are no words to explain how hard and amazing it was; it felt like I was ripped apart and slowly put back together anew. When I see the photos or footage from the trip, it's hard to believe I actually did that.

When I think about the trip, key moments come to my mind—like the time Jack and I almost got attacked by a grizzly bear in Canada, but we intimidated him by making a lot of noise, or the time I spent three days in the Yukon in a music festival, which I managed to do for free by saying I was a journalist.

One day, three teenagers with knives stole my film camera, but that turned out to be a blessing because we were able to get a better camera with the insurance money. Another day, we spent a couple of hours chasing whales in a boat off the coast of Mexico.

We were also part of the biggest Easter celebration in the world in Guatemala, and to this day I haven't seen a bigger crowd. Another moment I remember is the time I cried when I saw a tree—after spending three months in a desert, seeing only sand day after day.

Every experience was intense—both the good and the bad. The lows were extremely low, and the highs were extremely high.

One moment in our journey always comes first in my memory. By the time we got to Argentina, we were less than a month away from finishing our journey. We kept hearing that once we crossed to Argentina from Chile, we would face extreme weather conditions. People said the wind would be so strong that it would push us off our bicycles.

They were right: once we crossed over to Argentina, the wind was extremely powerful. But luckily for us, the wind was at our backs, so we were flying. In four hours, we rode the distance we would normally achieve in an entire day.

After a couple of days, the highway started to turn just enough for the wind to come at us sideways. And sure enough, it was pushing us constantly off our bicycles; we had to cycle at almost a 45-degree angle so we could stay upright.

A couple more days, and the highway started turning again. Suddenly, we had the wind blowing straight against us. That day was the windiest day of the season—we were battling an 80-mile-an-hour wind.

That's a hard experience to explain with words. It feels like there's a massive invisible force pushing you constantly, blocking you from moving forward. It's hard to overcome an obstacle you can't see.

The wind was so powerful that every part of my body was shaking. The entire bicycle was shaking. It was so loud that my ears hurt. It felt like a hundred people were screaming at me at the same time. It was so cold that every uncovered part of my body was burning. And I was so tired I couldn't even focus my eyes.

We battled the wind for five hours. It was exhausting. For a while I was screaming as hard as I could—that made me feel better. I felt furious, sad, terrified, and finally hopeless. I found myself asking God to please stop, but He didn't, and neither did I.

It's my nature to find ways to mentally cope with such situations, like daydreaming that I'm somewhere else. I imagined I wasn't there; I tried to convince myself that I wasn't hungry, or cold, or exhausted. I tried to convince myself that I wasn't in pain.

But then I thought about Marcy. I thought about her beautiful eyes and smile, and I remembered what she said: "You need to learn to love the pain, because that's where your love is needed the most."

It was then I decided to be there in the moment, to be present. I stopped wishing that I wasn't there and decided to pay attention. I decided to embrace the pain and just let things be. I decided to stop wishing for a better life, and to just *experience* my life instead. At that moment I felt a calm sense of peace. And just for a moment I felt closer to God, because for a moment, I accepted His will.

We get to decide whether pain is going to push us down or push us forward. We get to decide how we experience pain, and how it affects us on a daily basis. More importantly, we get to decide to be present, take charge, and live our lives.

The last day of riding, we woke up to a massive snowstorm—we were riding our bicycles while we were trying to eat snowflakes. We turned what could have been one of the worst days during our journey into one of the most beautiful ones.

After 21 months, we finally got to our destination—Ushuaia, Argentina, the southern tip of the Americas and the bottom of the world. That was the day I accomplished what seemed impossible. A couple of years before the trip, I couldn't even walk, and that day I had just cycled the world from top to bottom.

For years, I had thought about the moment we would be in Ushuaia. There would be a big party, I thought. Our friends and family would be waiting for us with big smiles on their faces, holding signs. The media would be taking photos and interviewing us. As in any movie, I thought there would be a big climax to our story. But our story wasn't a movie—at least not yet—and there was no big finale.

The day we finished our journey, it was just my three teammates and I, together, at the edge of the world. Just the four of us, and our bicycles.

We walked down to where the world ends, and just like we had done in the Arctic Ocean, we officially ended our journey by dunking our bicycles in the Antarctic Ocean. We hugged as a team, and sat down to look at the sunset. That moment is branded in my heart. It was beautiful, and I will never forget it.

It was then I realized that it was never about the destination. It was never about getting to the bottom of the world, but about everything that had happened *in between* Alaska and Argentina. To me, it was about everything that had happened since I left home—all the incredible landscapes I got to see along the way, all the amazing people who I got to learn from during the last couple of decades. It was about what the journey taught me, about how much I grew mentally, physically, emotionally, and spiritually.

It was about learning to love the pain. About loving every time I was hungry, cold, or tired. Loving every time I hesitated, or doubted that I was going to accomplish my dreams. Loving the times when I almost gave up, and even the times when I did.

The point of the journey was about loving the times I thought I had nothing more to give, when I actually did. Each one of those moments that came from pain were the moments that helped me know myself. More importantly, those were the moments that helped me conquer myself.

Chapter
– Nine –
Everything is Temporary

After 21 months together, the four of us needed some time on our own. I for sure needed it, since I could no longer focus. I would get a headache as soon as someone started talking to me. Anything and everything overwhelmed me; it felt like my brain had run on overdrive for such a long time. The only thing to do about it was to rest for a couple of months.

We heard about a meditation retreat outside of Buenos Aires where you had to meditate 10 hours a day for 10 days. During that time you had to be in complete silence—you couldn't communicate in any shape or form with anyone. No talking, no sign language, no blinking, no nothing. The purpose was for you to completely focus solely on your meditation practice.

They took your phone away, and you weren't allowed to read, write, exercise, or do anything else that wasn't meditating. I guess you could walk during breaks, but that's about it. Alcohol, drugs, and sex were completely out of the question. The whole point was to feel completely isolated during the retreat.

As weird as it sounds, that all actually sounded amazing to me. Complete isolation was exactly what I needed.

The retreat was held in a farm on the outskirts of Buenos Aires. About 70 of us were there, and we slept in a big warehouse. Men and women were evenly split into two sections, and we each had our own beds. We weren't allowed to interact with the other sex until the last day of the retreat.

Every day we would wake up at 4 a.m., meditate for a couple hours, have breakfast, and take a one-hour break. Then we would meditate for another three hours, have lunch, and another break. We would go back to meditate for another three hours, have tea, and then take our final break. After that, we would meditate one more time for a couple of hours.

It seems that I always find a way to get myself in extreme situations. Just writing about the retreat makes me uncomfortable. I honestly can't remember how I was able to do it. There were times I wanted to quit, but didn't. At least a couple of people left the meditation retreat halfway through. I wish they hadn't, because it definitely felt like a process that needed to last a full 10 days.

The meditation technique we followed—Vipassana meditation—was by far the most simple and powerful one I've ever done. For the entire time, we were to only focus our meditation on the sensations of our bodies. That's it. We would focus on what we were feeling on top of our heads—cold, warmth, tingling, pressure, or any other sensation. Then we would shift our focus an inch over, and we would concentrate on what sensation we felt there. We would do this throughout our entire bodies, inch by inch, backwards and forwards. For the entire 10 hours of meditation, we only focused on how we were feeling.

The retreat leaders explained that most meditation techniques focus on trying to quiet the mind, but that's a mistake. Instead of trying to quiet a mind that isn't naturally at peace, if we focus on *purifying* the mind, the quietness will come naturally.

You can purify the mind by focusing and releasing the sensations in your body. Vipassana meditation is about self-transformation by self-observation. The philosophy is that through this technique we can get to the root of our problems, and extract them from where they originated.

We learned two main teachings from this practice. First, everything is temporary. The way we learned that was by realizing that each one of the sensations we felt in our bodies was eventually going to go away. Second, no matter what happens, we should stay equanimous—centered and balanced. The way we learned that was by deciding to be unaffected, whether we felt a pleasant sensation or a repulsive one.

The goal was to experience the sensation for what it was. Not to push it away or hold on to it, but instead to let it take its natural course through our bodies. Learning that made me think of the time I had the pinched nerve in my back. It made me wonder whether the problem was that I held on to my pain instead of letting it take its natural course.

The retreat leaders also told us that impurity would present itself in the form of discomfort. I guess I was very impure, because it was very uncomfortable. Once again, the problem presented itself through my knees, which for the first couple of days were in extreme pain. Ideally, we were supposed to hold a sitting position with our legs crossed. I could barely hold that position before I had to change to a different one.

The purifying process brought the worst part of me to the surface. One night, I had an extremely dark and terrifying nightmare. My mom and I were arguing, I don't remember exactly about what. The argument escalated to the point where I was screaming furiously at her. At that moment I felt rage and an uncontrollable wrath. I felt something evil within me.

The inner commotion woke me up, and I immediately felt bad. I couldn't believe I was capable of so much anger and hate. It really shook me to think that I could feel that hatred for anyone—but especially my mom—even if it was just a dream.

That was just the beginning. Every time I took a nap or went to bed for the next couple of days, I had terrifying nightmares. It really felt like this meditation technique was bringing my impurities to the surface.

During the day, random flashes would appear in my mind. Out of nowhere, I would see images of death, hate, and darkness. It really concerned me, because that had never happened to me before. I thought maybe that was what people experienced when they went insane—or maybe because they were already crazy.

Not being able to talk to anyone about it made it worse. I felt very isolated and lonely. The only person we were allowed to talk to was the meditation guide. Every day after lunch he could answer any questions that we had. One day, I approached him.

"Mr. Miyagi," I said (using the nickname I gave him), "I feel like you opened a door that I'm not sure you can close." I told him I felt like I was going crazy, and that I was really concerned about it.

"What are the two main lessons of Vipassana?" he asked calmly.

"Everything is temporary, and you should stay equanimous no matter what," I replied.

He nodded and stayed quiet. I looked at him, trying to figure out what he meant. Was that it? I mean, I was about to have a mental breakdown, and his response pretty was much just, "Chill. It will pass."

I tried to argue, to convince him that my situation was more delicate than that, but he stood his ground. He told me that no situation was different, and that I should stay centered and balanced no matter what, because it was temporary.

"It's part of the process," he said. I left that meeting feeling really uncertain, but decided to follow his instructions.

A couple of days after my conversation with Mr. Miyagi, the flashes and nightmares stopped. Just like that, they were gone, and I was sleeping like a baby. In a way, it felt like I'd had an exorcism. I felt so light, so happy, so peaceful. It was like the nightmares and flashes in my head had never happened. I could hold my sitting position longer, and the pain in my knees was gone too. It felt like I was not only purifying my mind, but my body, too.

By the time the meditation retreat was done, I felt like I had gone through some kind of transformation. It was not only exactly what I wanted, but what I needed, too. I felt rejuvenated. It felt like all the pain, suffering, and struggles that had weighed me down during the 21-month journey had gone away. I felt happy for no reason, and that is a lot to say.

Chapter
— Ten —
A New Dream

Before I came back to the U.S., I spent some time with my family in Mexico. Just like I had done when I finished the pilgrimage, I needed to take some time to transition to my new life. It was good be in one place for more than a week. It was even better to be in a place that felt like home. There is something really beautiful about spending time with people who saw you grow up.

Finally, after two years, I came back to Austin, Texas. I think the hardest part of it was to come back to what supposedly was home. My teammates and I didn't have a place to stay, since we had left everything when we embarked on our journey. So "home" only meant a city where we once had lived, and it had changed a lot since we left. But more importantly, *we* had changed a lot since we left.

The first couple of months, it was very difficult to adjust. Once I found a place to live, it was hard to sleep in the same bed every night. A lot of times I wanted to put my hammock outside—I missed falling asleep while looking at the stars. It was odd feeling disconnected with nature. It didn't feel natural. It felt so weird sleeping between four walls with fake air blowing in your face.

For a while, I felt useless. I had spent the last two years focusing on accomplishing the hardest project I'd ever been a part of, and suddenly that extreme focus was gone. It made me feel lost. It also made me wonder whether everything I had learned during our journey could be applied in real life.

It took me months to be able to go to public places where there were a lot of people—I would get so claustrophobic. My girlfriend would invite me to go to the gym or do yoga, and I would tell her it was the last thing I wanted to do.

At the same time, with the completion of our project came the end of a dream. Pedal South represented everything I had worked for the last couple of decades. I got to travel the world, do what I love, and help people along the way. After all the sacrifices, all the pain and suffering, and all the loneliness, I finally got to fulfill my dream.

With that achievement came a sense of peace I had never felt before. Having a massive dream comes at a great expense. Part of the drive comes from the dream itself, from the love of it. The other part comes from the fear that your dream might not come true.

So for almost two decades, my dream fueled a massive unstoppable drive. And for almost two decades, I was in constant fear, because I didn't know if I was going to make it or not. That fear disappeared when I came back to the U.S.

But once the peace came, I found that my drive was gone. I spent most of my life pursuing something, and once I got to where I wanted to go, my drive was no longer needed. I was worried for a while, and I felt scared. I felt lost.

A friend asked me once how I was able to go after my dream with so much determination. He asked if I ever felt fear. I told him of course I did—I was just more afraid of *not* pursuing my dream than I was of pursuing it. I told him that if I hadn't gone after my dream, I wouldn't have found out who I was. My dream was the only thing that made sense to me, and without it I was lost.

After I spent time thinking about all the things I had learned during the previous two decades, I started to realize I had so much to share. I had gained so much knowledge and wisdom. I realized that for the last two decades I had been focusing on exploring and absorbing as much as I could, and now it was time to serve others by sharing everything I had learned along the way.

Winn told me "do it for someone else," and now is the time to pay it forward. Not just for "someone," but for as many people as I can.

Serving others is my new dream, and I could not have a greater one. With that new dream, my drive came back. But this time, instead of being fueled by fear, it's fueled by love.

My hope is that somehow and somewhere, people will hear my story and some of the things I learned along the way. I believe that some will be able to find their own strength within mine. Maybe some will find their own faith within mine. I don't think that my way is the only way, but I found my own, and I want other people to find theirs.

Even though I accomplished what I set out to do, I still wonder about my future—whether I'll accomplish my greatest dream of serving others. I imagine what it will be like when I encounter God, just before He claims back his spark of life that I call spirit. I wonder what I will say. I envision the moment when I start melting and little by little I become one with Him.

Just before I lose the concept of separation from my Creator, I will humbly ask Him one last thing:

"Please send me back. Please give me another chance. Please, let me experience the gift of life one more time."

THANK YOU SO MUCH FOR TAKING THE TIME TO read my story. I hope it made a difference in your life. If it has, please share it with someone else who might need it.

I really appreciate all your feedback, and I love hearing what you have to say, so please give this book a review on Amazon here:

<https://goo.gl/9Kkfye>.

God bless you.
Ricardo

Let's Work Together

If you'd like to learn more about what I've experienced in a personal one-on-one setting, I offer personal coaching. I can help you bet on yourself: clarify your purpose, achieve what seems impossible, become a powerful, mindful leader, and—most importantly—love the journey.

If you'd like me to speak to your organization, I offer custom-tailored keynote speeches. I work closely with you to understand your organization's specific needs, and I will motivate your audience to be more effective, efficient, and productive. My unique experience allows me to teach others how to unlock their potential, achieve what seems impossible, and learn to love the journey.

I limit my schedule to just a few keynote speeches a month, so I can give your event my undivided attention.

Please visit my website for more information on what I offer and how to contact me:

ricardopal.com

Made in the USA
Columbia, SC
01 October 2024